50 A World of Salads Recipes

By: Kelly Johnson

Table of Contents

- Mediterranean Quinoa Salad
- Classic Caesar Salad
- Thai Mango Salad
- Greek Village Salad
- Caprese Salad with Balsamic Glaze
- Roasted Beet and Goat Cheese Salad
- Asian Sesame Noodle Salad
- Cobb Salad
- Warm Potato Salad with Bacon
- Avocado and Black Bean Salad
- Southwest Chicken Salad
- Shaved Brussels Sprout Salad
- Chickpea and Cucumber Salad
- Waldorf Salad
- Spicy Kimchi Salad
- Smoked Salmon and Arugula Salad
- Curried Carrot and Raisin Salad
- Roasted Sweet Potato and Kale Salad
- Grilled Peach and Burrata Salad
- Spinach and Strawberry Salad
- Chicken Caesar Pasta Salad
- Panzanella (Italian Bread Salad)
- Raw Zucchini and Tomato Salad
- Quinoa Tabbouleh Salad
- Miso Cucumber and Avocado Salad
- Green Bean and Almond Salad
- Watermelon and Feta Salad
- Roasted Cauliflower Salad with Tahini Dressing
- Cabbage and Apple Slaw
- Grilled Shrimp and Mango Salad
- Roasted Chickpea and Spinach Salad
- Beetroot and Orange Salad
- Apple and Walnut Salad with Blue Cheese
- Asian Cabbage Salad with Peanut Dressing
- Roasted Carrot and Lentil Salad

- Kale and Roasted Squash Salad
- Couscous Salad with Dried Fruit and Nuts
- Tuna Nicoise Salad
- Marinated Tomato Salad
- Warm Farro and Roasted Mushroom Salad
- Chopped Salad with Balsamic Dressing
- Avocado, Tomato, and Cucumber Salad
- Grilled Vegetable Salad
- Smoked Turkey and Cranberry Salad
- Sweet Potato and Kale Salad with Maple Dressing
- Arugula, Pear, and Pecan Salad
- Roasted Root Vegetable Salad
- Broccoli and Feta Salad
- Apple Cider Vinegar Slaw
- Poppy Seed Coleslaw

Mediterranean Quinoa Salad

Ingredients:

- 1 cup quinoa, cooked and cooled
- 1 cup cherry tomatoes, halved
- 1 cucumber, diced
- 1/2 red onion, finely chopped
- 1/4 cup Kalamata olives, pitted and sliced
- 1/4 cup feta cheese, crumbled
- 1/4 cup fresh parsley, chopped
- 2 tbsp olive oil
- 1 tbsp lemon juice
- 1 tsp dried oregano
- Salt and pepper to taste

Instructions:

1. In a large bowl, combine the cooked quinoa, cherry tomatoes, cucumber, red onion, olives, feta, and parsley.
2. In a small bowl, whisk together the olive oil, lemon juice, oregano, salt, and pepper.
3. Pour the dressing over the salad and toss gently to combine. Serve chilled or at room temperature.

Classic Caesar Salad

Ingredients:

- 6 cups romaine lettuce, chopped
- 1 cup croutons
- 1/2 cup grated Parmesan cheese
- 1/4 cup Caesar dressing (store-bought or homemade)

For the Caesar dressing (optional):

- 1/2 cup mayonnaise
- 2 tbsp Dijon mustard
- 1 tbsp lemon juice
- 1 tbsp anchovy paste or 2 anchovy fillets, mashed
- 1 garlic clove, minced
- 1/2 tsp Worcestershire sauce
- Salt and pepper to taste

Instructions:

1. For the dressing, whisk together mayonnaise, mustard, lemon juice, anchovy paste, garlic, Worcestershire sauce, salt, and pepper. Adjust seasoning to taste.
2. In a large bowl, toss the romaine lettuce with the Caesar dressing until well-coated.
3. Add croutons and Parmesan cheese, and toss gently. Serve immediately.

Thai Mango Salad

Ingredients:

- 2 ripe mangoes, peeled and julienned
- 1 cup shredded carrots
- 1/2 red bell pepper, thinly sliced
- 1/2 cucumber, julienned
- 1/4 cup fresh cilantro, chopped
- 2 tbsp crushed peanuts (optional)
- 1 tbsp sesame seeds (optional)

For the dressing:

- 2 tbsp fish sauce
- 1 tbsp lime juice
- 1 tbsp honey or sugar
- 1 tbsp rice vinegar
- 1 tsp chili flakes (optional)

Instructions:

1. In a large bowl, combine the mangoes, carrots, bell pepper, cucumber, and cilantro.
2. For the dressing, whisk together fish sauce, lime juice, honey, rice vinegar, and chili flakes (if using).
3. Drizzle the dressing over the salad and toss gently. Garnish with crushed peanuts and sesame seeds if desired.

Greek Village Salad

Ingredients:

- 2 large tomatoes, cut into wedges
- 1 cucumber, sliced
- 1/2 red onion, thinly sliced
- 1/4 cup Kalamata olives, pitted
- 1/2 cup feta cheese, block or crumbled
- 1 tbsp dried oregano
- 1/4 cup olive oil
- 2 tbsp red wine vinegar
- Salt and pepper to taste

Instructions:

1. In a large bowl, combine the tomatoes, cucumber, red onion, olives, and feta.
2. Sprinkle the dried oregano over the salad and drizzle with olive oil and red wine vinegar.
3. Season with salt and pepper, and toss gently to combine. Serve immediately.

Caprese Salad with Balsamic Glaze

Ingredients:

- 4 large ripe tomatoes, sliced
- 8 oz fresh mozzarella cheese, sliced
- 1/4 cup fresh basil leaves
- 2 tbsp olive oil
- 2 tbsp balsamic glaze
- Salt and pepper to taste

Instructions:

1. Arrange the tomato and mozzarella slices in an alternating pattern on a serving platter.
2. Tuck fresh basil leaves in between the tomato and mozzarella.
3. Drizzle with olive oil and balsamic glaze, then season with salt and pepper.
4. Serve immediately or chill for a short time before serving.

Roasted Beet and Goat Cheese Salad

Ingredients:

- 3 medium beets, roasted and peeled, sliced
- 4 cups mixed greens (arugula, spinach, or a spring mix)
- 1/2 cup goat cheese, crumbled
- 1/4 cup candied walnuts or pecans
- 1/4 cup balsamic vinaigrette dressing

Instructions:

1. Preheat the oven to 400°F (200°C). Wrap the beets in aluminum foil and roast for 45 minutes to 1 hour, or until tender. Let cool, peel, and slice.
2. In a large bowl, toss the mixed greens with the roasted beets, goat cheese, and candied nuts.
3. Drizzle with balsamic vinaigrette and toss gently. Serve immediately.

Asian Sesame Noodle Salad

Ingredients:

- 8 oz rice noodles or soba noodles, cooked and cooled
- 1/2 red bell pepper, julienned
- 1/2 cucumber, julienned
- 2 tbsp sesame seeds
- 1/4 cup green onions, chopped
- 2 tbsp cilantro, chopped

For the dressing:

- 2 tbsp soy sauce
- 1 tbsp sesame oil
- 1 tbsp rice vinegar
- 1 tbsp honey
- 1 tsp ginger, grated
- 1 clove garlic, minced
- 1/2 tsp chili flakes (optional)

Instructions:

1. In a large bowl, combine the noodles, red bell pepper, cucumber, sesame seeds, green onions, and cilantro.
2. For the dressing, whisk together soy sauce, sesame oil, rice vinegar, honey, ginger, garlic, and chili flakes.
3. Drizzle the dressing over the salad and toss to coat. Serve chilled or at room temperature.

Cobb Salad

Ingredients:

- 4 cups mixed salad greens (such as Romaine, spinach, or iceberg)
- 1 chicken breast, grilled and sliced
- 2 boiled eggs, chopped
- 1 avocado, sliced
- 1/2 cup cherry tomatoes, halved
- 1/4 cup crumbled blue cheese
- 1/4 cup cooked bacon, crumbled
- 1/4 cup red onion, sliced

For the dressing:

- 1/4 cup olive oil
- 1 tbsp red wine vinegar
- 1 tsp Dijon mustard
- Salt and pepper to taste

Instructions:

1. Arrange the mixed greens on a large platter or in individual bowls.
2. Layer the chicken, eggs, avocado, tomatoes, blue cheese, bacon, and red onion on top of the greens.
3. In a small bowl, whisk together the olive oil, red wine vinegar, Dijon mustard, salt, and pepper.
4. Drizzle the dressing over the salad and serve immediately.

Warm Potato Salad with Bacon

Ingredients:

- 2 lbs small new potatoes, halved or quartered
- 6 slices bacon, chopped
- 1/2 red onion, thinly sliced
- 1/4 cup fresh parsley, chopped
- 2 tbsp Dijon mustard
- 3 tbsp olive oil
- 2 tbsp apple cider vinegar
- Salt and pepper to taste

Instructions:

1. In a large pot, boil the potatoes until tender, about 15-20 minutes. Drain and set aside.
2. In a skillet, cook the chopped bacon over medium heat until crispy. Remove and set aside on paper towels to drain.
3. In the same skillet, sauté the red onion in the bacon fat until soft, about 2-3 minutes.
4. In a small bowl, whisk together the Dijon mustard, olive oil, apple cider vinegar, salt, and pepper.
5. In a large bowl, toss the cooked potatoes with the sautéed onion, bacon, and dressing. Garnish with fresh parsley and serve warm.

Avocado and Black Bean Salad

Ingredients:

- 2 ripe avocados, diced
- 1 can (15 oz) black beans, drained and rinsed
- 1/2 red onion, finely chopped
- 1 red bell pepper, diced
- 1/4 cup fresh cilantro, chopped
- 1 tbsp lime juice
- 2 tbsp olive oil
- Salt and pepper to taste

Instructions:

1. In a large bowl, combine the diced avocados, black beans, red onion, bell pepper, and cilantro.
2. Drizzle with lime juice and olive oil. Season with salt and pepper to taste.
3. Gently toss the salad and serve immediately, or refrigerate for up to 1 hour before serving.

Southwest Chicken Salad

Ingredients:

- 2 chicken breasts, grilled and sliced
- 4 cups mixed greens (such as Romaine, spinach, and arugula)
- 1 cup corn kernels (fresh, frozen, or canned)
- 1 red bell pepper, diced
- 1/2 red onion, thinly sliced
- 1/2 cup shredded cheddar cheese
- 1/4 cup fresh cilantro, chopped
- 1/4 cup tortilla chips, crushed (optional)

For the dressing:

- 1/4 cup olive oil
- 2 tbsp lime juice
- 1 tbsp honey
- 1 tsp chili powder
- Salt and pepper to taste

Instructions:

1. In a large bowl, combine the mixed greens, corn, bell pepper, red onion, cheddar cheese, and cilantro.
2. For the dressing, whisk together olive oil, lime juice, honey, chili powder, salt, and pepper.
3. Toss the salad with the dressing and top with the grilled chicken slices. Garnish with crushed tortilla chips and serve.

Shaved Brussels Sprout Salad

Ingredients:

- 1 lb Brussels sprouts, trimmed and thinly sliced
- 1/4 cup toasted almonds, chopped
- 1/4 cup dried cranberries
- 1/2 cup Parmesan cheese, shaved
- 2 tbsp olive oil
- 1 tbsp lemon juice
- Salt and pepper to taste

Instructions:

1. In a large bowl, toss the thinly sliced Brussels sprouts with olive oil and lemon juice.
2. Add the toasted almonds, dried cranberries, and Parmesan cheese. Toss again.
3. Season with salt and pepper to taste. Serve immediately or let sit for 10-15 minutes to let the flavors meld.

Chickpea and Cucumber Salad

Ingredients:

- 1 can (15 oz) chickpeas, drained and rinsed
- 1 cucumber, diced
- 1/2 red onion, thinly sliced
- 1/4 cup fresh parsley, chopped
- 2 tbsp olive oil
- 1 tbsp red wine vinegar
- Salt and pepper to taste

Instructions:

1. In a large bowl, combine the chickpeas, cucumber, red onion, and parsley.
2. Drizzle with olive oil and red wine vinegar, then season with salt and pepper.
3. Toss gently to combine and serve chilled or at room temperature.

Waldorf Salad

Ingredients:

- 2 cups diced apples (about 2 medium apples)
- 1 cup celery, chopped
- 1/2 cup grapes, halved
- 1/2 cup walnuts, chopped
- 1/2 cup Greek yogurt or mayonnaise
- 1 tbsp honey
- 1 tbsp lemon juice
- Salt and pepper to taste

Instructions:

1. In a large bowl, combine the apples, celery, grapes, and walnuts.
2. In a small bowl, mix together the yogurt (or mayonnaise), honey, lemon juice, salt, and pepper.
3. Pour the dressing over the salad and toss gently to combine. Serve immediately or refrigerate for up to an hour.

Spicy Kimchi Salad

Ingredients:

- 2 cups kimchi, chopped
- 1/2 cucumber, julienned
- 1/4 red onion, thinly sliced
- 1/4 cup fresh cilantro, chopped
- 2 tbsp sesame oil
- 1 tbsp rice vinegar
- 1 tbsp soy sauce
- 1 tsp gochugaru (Korean chili flakes) or red pepper flakes
- 1 tbsp sesame seeds (optional)

Instructions:

1. In a large bowl, combine the kimchi, cucumber, red onion, and cilantro.
2. In a small bowl, whisk together the sesame oil, rice vinegar, soy sauce, gochugaru (or red pepper flakes), and sesame seeds (if using).
3. Drizzle the dressing over the salad and toss gently. Serve immediately or chill for 30 minutes for extra flavor.

Smoked Salmon and Arugula Salad

Ingredients:

- 4 oz smoked salmon, torn into pieces
- 4 cups arugula
- 1/2 red onion, thinly sliced
- 1/2 avocado, sliced
- 2 tbsp capers
- 1 tbsp olive oil
- 1 tbsp lemon juice
- Salt and pepper to taste

Instructions:

1. In a large bowl, combine the arugula, smoked salmon, red onion, avocado, and capers.
2. Drizzle with olive oil and lemon juice, then season with salt and pepper.
3. Toss gently to combine and serve immediately.

Curried Carrot and Raisin Salad

Ingredients:

- 4 medium carrots, grated
- 1/2 cup raisins
- 1/4 cup mayonnaise or Greek yogurt
- 1 tbsp curry powder
- 1 tbsp honey
- 1 tbsp lemon juice
- Salt and pepper to taste

Instructions:

1. In a large bowl, combine the grated carrots and raisins.
2. In a separate small bowl, whisk together the mayonnaise (or yogurt), curry powder, honey, and lemon juice.
3. Pour the dressing over the carrot and raisin mixture and toss to combine.
4. Season with salt and pepper to taste. Chill for 30 minutes before serving for best flavor.

Roasted Sweet Potato and Kale Salad

Ingredients:

- 2 large sweet potatoes, peeled and cubed
- 4 cups kale, chopped
- 1 tbsp olive oil
- 1 tsp cumin
- 1/2 tsp paprika
- Salt and pepper to taste
- 1/4 cup crumbled feta cheese (optional)
- 1/4 cup pumpkin seeds or sunflower seeds
- 2 tbsp balsamic vinegar

Instructions:

1. Preheat the oven to 400°F (200°C). Toss the sweet potato cubes with olive oil, cumin, paprika, salt, and pepper.
2. Spread the sweet potatoes on a baking sheet and roast for 25-30 minutes, or until tender and slightly caramelized, flipping halfway through.
3. In a large bowl, massage the kale with a little olive oil and balsamic vinegar until it softens.
4. Add the roasted sweet potatoes to the kale, then top with feta and seeds. Toss gently and serve warm or at room temperature.

Grilled Peach and Burrata Salad

Ingredients:

- 2 ripe peaches, halved and pitted
- 8 oz burrata cheese
- 4 cups mixed greens (such as arugula and spinach)
- 1 tbsp honey
- 1 tbsp olive oil
- Salt and pepper to taste
- Fresh basil leaves for garnish

Instructions:

1. Preheat the grill to medium heat. Brush the peach halves with olive oil and grill for 3-4 minutes per side, until slightly charred and softened.
2. Arrange the mixed greens on a platter and top with grilled peaches and burrata.
3. Drizzle honey and olive oil over the salad. Season with salt and pepper, then garnish with fresh basil leaves.
4. Serve immediately for a fresh and savory-sweet salad.

Spinach and Strawberry Salad

Ingredients:

- 4 cups fresh spinach, washed and dried
- 1 cup strawberries, sliced
- 1/4 cup red onion, thinly sliced
- 1/4 cup toasted almonds or walnuts
- 2 tbsp balsamic vinegar
- 2 tbsp olive oil
- 1 tsp honey
- Salt and pepper to taste

Instructions:

1. In a large bowl, combine the spinach, strawberries, red onion, and toasted nuts.
2. In a small bowl, whisk together the balsamic vinegar, olive oil, honey, salt, and pepper.
3. Pour the dressing over the salad and toss gently to combine. Serve immediately.

Chicken Caesar Pasta Salad

Ingredients:

- 2 cups cooked rotini or penne pasta
- 2 cups cooked chicken breast, shredded
- 1/2 cup Caesar dressing
- 1/4 cup grated Parmesan cheese
- 1/2 cup croutons
- 1/4 cup fresh parsley, chopped
- Salt and pepper to taste

Instructions:

1. In a large bowl, combine the pasta and shredded chicken.
2. Toss with Caesar dressing and Parmesan cheese until evenly coated.
3. Add croutons, parsley, and season with salt and pepper to taste.
4. Chill in the fridge for 30 minutes before serving for best flavor.

Panzanella (Italian Bread Salad)

Ingredients:

- 4 cups cubed stale bread (preferably sourdough or baguette)
- 2 cups ripe tomatoes, chopped
- 1 cucumber, diced
- 1/2 red onion, thinly sliced
- 1/4 cup fresh basil, torn
- 2 tbsp red wine vinegar
- 1/4 cup olive oil
- Salt and pepper to taste

Instructions:

1. Preheat the oven to 375°F (190°C). Spread the cubed bread on a baking sheet and toast in the oven for about 10 minutes, or until golden and crispy.
2. In a large bowl, combine the toasted bread, tomatoes, cucumber, red onion, and basil.
3. Drizzle with red wine vinegar and olive oil, and season with salt and pepper.
4. Toss the salad well and let it sit for 20 minutes before serving to allow the flavors to meld.

Raw Zucchini and Tomato Salad

Ingredients:

- 2 medium zucchinis, thinly sliced
- 2 cups cherry tomatoes, halved
- 1/4 cup red onion, thinly sliced
- 1/4 cup fresh basil, chopped
- 2 tbsp olive oil
- 1 tbsp lemon juice
- Salt and pepper to taste

Instructions:

1. In a large bowl, combine the zucchini, tomatoes, red onion, and basil.
2. Drizzle with olive oil and lemon juice. Toss gently to combine.
3. Season with salt and pepper to taste. Serve immediately or refrigerate for up to 30 minutes before serving.

Quinoa Tabbouleh Salad

Ingredients:

- 1 cup quinoa, cooked and cooled
- 1 cup fresh parsley, chopped
- 1/2 cup fresh mint, chopped
- 1 cucumber, diced
- 2 tomatoes, diced
- 1/4 cup red onion, finely chopped
- 2 tbsp olive oil
- 2 tbsp lemon juice
- Salt and pepper to taste

Instructions:

1. In a large bowl, combine the cooked quinoa, parsley, mint, cucumber, tomatoes, and red onion.
2. Drizzle with olive oil and lemon juice, then toss to combine.
3. Season with salt and pepper to taste, and serve chilled or at room temperature.

Miso Cucumber and Avocado Salad

Ingredients:

- 2 large cucumbers, sliced
- 1 avocado, diced
- 2 tbsp white miso paste
- 1 tbsp rice vinegar
- 1 tbsp sesame oil
- 1 tbsp soy sauce
- 1 tsp honey
- 1 tbsp sesame seeds (optional)
- Fresh cilantro for garnish (optional)

Instructions:

1. In a bowl, whisk together the miso paste, rice vinegar, sesame oil, soy sauce, and honey to create the dressing.
2. In a large bowl, combine the sliced cucumbers and diced avocado.
3. Pour the miso dressing over the cucumber and avocado, and toss gently to coat.
4. Sprinkle with sesame seeds and garnish with cilantro before serving.

Green Bean and Almond Salad

Ingredients:

- 4 cups green beans, trimmed
- 1/4 cup sliced almonds
- 1 tbsp olive oil
- 1 tbsp lemon juice
- 1 tsp Dijon mustard
- Salt and pepper to taste
- Fresh parsley for garnish

Instructions:

1. Bring a pot of salted water to a boil and cook the green beans for 3-4 minutes until tender-crisp. Drain and rinse under cold water to stop the cooking process.
2. Toast the sliced almonds in a dry skillet over medium heat until golden and fragrant.
3. In a small bowl, whisk together the olive oil, lemon juice, Dijon mustard, salt, and pepper.
4. In a large bowl, combine the green beans, toasted almonds, and dressing. Toss to combine and garnish with fresh parsley.

Watermelon and Feta Salad

Ingredients:

- 4 cups cubed watermelon
- 1/2 cup crumbled feta cheese
- 1/4 cup fresh mint, chopped
- 1 tbsp olive oil
- 1 tbsp lime juice
- Salt and pepper to taste

Instructions:

1. In a large bowl, combine the cubed watermelon, crumbled feta, and chopped mint.
2. Drizzle with olive oil and lime juice, and toss gently.
3. Season with salt and pepper to taste. Serve chilled.

Roasted Cauliflower Salad with Tahini Dressing

Ingredients:

- 1 medium cauliflower, cut into florets
- 2 tbsp olive oil
- 1/2 tsp cumin
- Salt and pepper to taste
- 1/4 cup tahini
- 2 tbsp lemon juice
- 1 tbsp water (to thin the dressing)
- 2 tbsp fresh parsley, chopped
- 1/4 cup pomegranate seeds (optional)

Instructions:

1. Preheat the oven to 400°F (200°C). Toss the cauliflower florets with olive oil, cumin, salt, and pepper. Spread on a baking sheet.
2. Roast the cauliflower for 20-25 minutes, or until golden and tender.
3. In a small bowl, whisk together the tahini, lemon juice, and water to create the dressing. Adjust with more water if necessary.
4. Once the cauliflower is done, toss it with the tahini dressing, and garnish with fresh parsley and pomegranate seeds before serving.

Cabbage and Apple Slaw

Ingredients:

- 4 cups shredded cabbage (green or purple)
- 1 large apple, julienned
- 1/4 cup shredded carrots
- 1/4 cup apple cider vinegar
- 2 tbsp olive oil
- 1 tbsp honey or maple syrup
- Salt and pepper to taste
- 1/4 cup chopped fresh parsley

Instructions:

1. In a large bowl, combine the shredded cabbage, apple slices, and shredded carrots.
2. In a separate bowl, whisk together the apple cider vinegar, olive oil, honey, salt, and pepper.
3. Pour the dressing over the cabbage mixture and toss to coat.
4. Garnish with fresh parsley before serving.

Grilled Shrimp and Mango Salad

Ingredients:

- 1 lb shrimp, peeled and deveined
- 1 ripe mango, diced
- 4 cups mixed greens (such as arugula or spinach)
- 1/4 red onion, thinly sliced
- 1 tbsp olive oil
- 1 tbsp lime juice
- Salt and pepper to taste
- Fresh cilantro for garnish

Instructions:

1. Preheat the grill to medium-high heat. Toss the shrimp with olive oil, lime juice, salt, and pepper.
2. Grill the shrimp for 2-3 minutes per side, until cooked through and pink.
3. In a large bowl, combine the mixed greens, diced mango, and red onion.
4. Add the grilled shrimp on top and garnish with fresh cilantro. Serve with a squeeze of lime juice.

Roasted Chickpea and Spinach Salad

Ingredients:

- 1 can (15 oz) chickpeas, drained and rinsed
- 1 tbsp olive oil
- 1 tsp smoked paprika
- 1/2 tsp cumin
- Salt and pepper to taste
- 4 cups spinach, washed and dried
- 1 tbsp tahini
- 1 tbsp lemon juice

Instructions:

1. Preheat the oven to 400°F (200°C). Toss the chickpeas with olive oil, smoked paprika, cumin, salt, and pepper.
2. Spread the chickpeas on a baking sheet and roast for 20-25 minutes, stirring halfway through, until crispy.
3. In a large bowl, toss the spinach with tahini and lemon juice.
4. Top the salad with the roasted chickpeas and serve immediately.

Beetroot and Orange Salad

Ingredients:

- 2 medium beets, cooked and peeled, sliced
- 2 oranges, peeled and segmented
- 1/4 cup red onion, thinly sliced
- 1/4 cup fresh mint, chopped
- 1 tbsp olive oil
- 1 tbsp balsamic vinegar
- Salt and pepper to taste

Instructions:

1. In a large bowl, combine the beet slices, orange segments, red onion, and mint.
2. Drizzle with olive oil and balsamic vinegar, and toss gently to combine.
3. Season with salt and pepper to taste and serve immediately.

Apple and Walnut Salad with Blue Cheese

Ingredients:

- 2 apples, thinly sliced
- 1/2 cup toasted walnuts
- 1/4 cup crumbled blue cheese
- 4 cups mixed greens (arugula, spinach, or baby kale)
- 2 tbsp olive oil
- 1 tbsp apple cider vinegar
- 1 tbsp honey
- Salt and pepper to taste

Instructions:

1. In a large bowl, combine the mixed greens, sliced apples, toasted walnuts, and crumbled blue cheese.
2. In a small bowl, whisk together the olive oil, apple cider vinegar, honey, salt, and pepper.
3. Drizzle the dressing over the salad and toss gently to combine. Serve immediately.

Asian Cabbage Salad with Peanut Dressing

Ingredients:

- 4 cups shredded cabbage (green or purple)
- 1/2 cup shredded carrots
- 1/4 cup green onions, chopped
- 1/4 cup toasted sesame seeds
- 1/4 cup cilantro, chopped
- 1 tbsp olive oil

For the Peanut Dressing:

- 1/4 cup peanut butter
- 2 tbsp soy sauce
- 1 tbsp rice vinegar
- 1 tbsp honey
- 1 tsp sesame oil
- 1 tsp grated ginger
- 1-2 tbsp water (to thin)

Instructions:

1. In a large bowl, combine the shredded cabbage, carrots, green onions, sesame seeds, and cilantro.
2. In a separate bowl, whisk together the peanut butter, soy sauce, rice vinegar, honey, sesame oil, grated ginger, and water to create the dressing.
3. Drizzle the dressing over the cabbage mixture and toss to coat evenly. Serve chilled or at room temperature.

Roasted Carrot and Lentil Salad

Ingredients:

- 3 large carrots, peeled and sliced into rounds
- 1 cup cooked lentils (green or brown)
- 1/4 cup olive oil
- 1 tbsp ground cumin
- 1 tbsp lemon juice
- 1/4 cup fresh parsley, chopped
- Salt and pepper to taste

Instructions:

1. Preheat the oven to 400°F (200°C). Toss the sliced carrots with 1 tablespoon olive oil, ground cumin, salt, and pepper. Spread the carrots on a baking sheet.
2. Roast the carrots for 20-25 minutes, until tender and slightly caramelized.
3. In a large bowl, combine the cooked lentils and roasted carrots. Drizzle with the remaining olive oil and lemon juice.
4. Toss to combine and garnish with chopped parsley. Serve warm or at room temperature.

Kale and Roasted Squash Salad

Ingredients:

- 2 cups cubed butternut squash
- 1 tbsp olive oil
- 1 tsp ground cinnamon
- 1/2 tsp ground nutmeg
- Salt and pepper to taste
- 4 cups kale, stems removed and chopped
- 1/4 cup feta cheese, crumbled
- 1/4 cup pumpkin seeds (optional)

For the Dressing:

- 2 tbsp olive oil
- 1 tbsp balsamic vinegar
- 1 tbsp honey
- Salt and pepper to taste

Instructions:

1. Preheat the oven to 400°F (200°C). Toss the cubed butternut squash with olive oil, cinnamon, nutmeg, salt, and pepper. Roast on a baking sheet for 20-25 minutes, or until tender and caramelized.
2. In a large bowl, massage the kale with olive oil and a pinch of salt until softened.
3. Once the squash is roasted, add it to the kale along with the feta cheese and pumpkin seeds.
4. In a small bowl, whisk together the balsamic vinegar, honey, and olive oil to make the dressing. Drizzle over the salad and toss gently to combine.

Couscous Salad with Dried Fruit and Nuts

Ingredients:

- 1 cup couscous
- 1/2 cup dried apricots, chopped
- 1/4 cup raisins or currants
- 1/4 cup toasted almonds, chopped
- 1/4 cup chopped fresh parsley
- 1 tbsp olive oil
- 1 tbsp lemon juice
- Salt and pepper to taste

Instructions:

1. Cook the couscous according to package instructions. Let it cool slightly.
2. In a large bowl, combine the couscous with the dried apricots, raisins, toasted almonds, and parsley.
3. Drizzle with olive oil and lemon juice, and season with salt and pepper. Toss to combine and serve.

Tuna Nicoise Salad

Ingredients:

- 2 cups mixed greens
- 1/2 lb small potatoes, boiled and halved
- 2 hard-boiled eggs, sliced
- 1/2 cup green beans, blanched
- 1/2 cup Kalamata olives
- 1 can (5 oz) tuna in olive oil, drained
- 1/4 cup cherry tomatoes, halved

For the Dressing:

- 2 tbsp olive oil
- 1 tbsp Dijon mustard
- 1 tbsp red wine vinegar
- 1 tsp lemon juice
- Salt and pepper to taste

Instructions:

1. In a large salad bowl, combine the mixed greens, potatoes, eggs, green beans, olives, tuna, and tomatoes.
2. In a small bowl, whisk together the olive oil, Dijon mustard, red wine vinegar, lemon juice, salt, and pepper to create the dressing.
3. Drizzle the dressing over the salad and toss gently to combine. Serve immediately.

Marinated Tomato Salad

Ingredients:

- 3 large tomatoes, sliced
- 1/2 red onion, thinly sliced
- 1/4 cup fresh basil, chopped
- 2 tbsp olive oil
- 1 tbsp red wine vinegar
- Salt and pepper to taste

Instructions:

1. In a bowl, layer the sliced tomatoes, red onion, and fresh basil.
2. Drizzle with olive oil and red wine vinegar, and season with salt and pepper.
3. Let the salad marinate for 30 minutes at room temperature before serving.

Warm Farro and Roasted Mushroom Salad

Ingredients:

- 1 cup farro, cooked
- 1 lb mushrooms (cremini or button), sliced
- 2 tbsp olive oil
- 1 tbsp balsamic vinegar
- 1/4 cup fresh parsley, chopped
- Salt and pepper to taste

Instructions:

1. Preheat the oven to 400°F (200°C). Toss the sliced mushrooms with 1 tablespoon olive oil, salt, and pepper. Roast for 15-20 minutes, until tender and browned.
2. In a large bowl, combine the cooked farro with the roasted mushrooms.
3. Drizzle with balsamic vinegar and the remaining olive oil. Toss gently and garnish with fresh parsley before serving.

Chopped Salad with Balsamic Dressing

Ingredients:

- 2 cups Romaine lettuce, chopped
- 1 cup cucumber, diced
- 1 cup bell pepper (red or yellow), diced
- 1/2 cup red onion, finely diced
- 1/2 cup cherry tomatoes, halved
- 1/2 cup Kalamata olives, pitted and chopped
- 1/4 cup feta cheese, crumbled
- Salt and pepper to taste

For the Balsamic Dressing:

- 3 tbsp balsamic vinegar
- 1/4 cup olive oil
- 1 tsp Dijon mustard
- 1 tsp honey
- Salt and pepper to taste

Instructions:

1. In a large bowl, combine the chopped Romaine lettuce, cucumber, bell pepper, red onion, cherry tomatoes, olives, and feta cheese.
2. In a separate small bowl, whisk together the balsamic vinegar, olive oil, Dijon mustard, honey, salt, and pepper to make the dressing.
3. Pour the dressing over the salad and toss until evenly coated. Serve immediately.

Avocado, Tomato, and Cucumber Salad

Ingredients:

- 2 ripe avocados, diced
- 1 cup cherry tomatoes, halved
- 1 cucumber, sliced
- 1/4 cup red onion, thinly sliced
- 1 tbsp fresh cilantro, chopped (optional)
- Salt and pepper to taste

For the Dressing:

- 2 tbsp olive oil
- 1 tbsp lime juice
- 1 tsp honey or agave syrup
- Salt and pepper to taste

Instructions:

1. In a large bowl, combine the diced avocados, cherry tomatoes, cucumber, and red onion.
2. In a small bowl, whisk together the olive oil, lime juice, honey, salt, and pepper to make the dressing.
3. Drizzle the dressing over the salad and toss gently to combine. Garnish with fresh cilantro (if using). Serve immediately.

Grilled Vegetable Salad

Ingredients:

- 1 zucchini, sliced into rounds
- 1 yellow squash, sliced into rounds
- 1 red bell pepper, cut into strips
- 1 red onion, cut into wedges
- 8 oz mushrooms, whole or halved
- 2 tbsp olive oil
- Salt and pepper to taste
- 2 tbsp fresh basil, chopped

For the Dressing:

- 3 tbsp olive oil
- 1 tbsp balsamic vinegar
- 1 tsp Dijon mustard
- 1 garlic clove, minced
- Salt and pepper to taste

Instructions:

1. Preheat the grill or grill pan to medium-high heat.
2. Toss the zucchini, yellow squash, bell pepper, onion, and mushrooms with olive oil, salt, and pepper.
3. Grill the vegetables for 4-5 minutes on each side until tender and lightly charred.
4. While the vegetables are grilling, whisk together the olive oil, balsamic vinegar, Dijon mustard, garlic, salt, and pepper to make the dressing.
5. Once the vegetables are grilled, place them on a large platter, drizzle with the dressing, and garnish with fresh basil. Serve warm or at room temperature.

Smoked Turkey and Cranberry Salad

Ingredients:

- 2 cups mixed greens (spinach, arugula, or baby kale)
- 1 cup smoked turkey breast, sliced or shredded
- 1/2 cup dried cranberries
- 1/4 cup walnuts, chopped
- 1/4 cup goat cheese or feta, crumbled
- 1/2 cup cucumber, sliced

For the Dressing:

- 2 tbsp olive oil
- 1 tbsp apple cider vinegar
- 1 tbsp Dijon mustard
- 1 tsp honey
- Salt and pepper to taste

Instructions:

1. In a large bowl, combine the mixed greens, smoked turkey, dried cranberries, walnuts, goat cheese, and cucumber.
2. In a small bowl, whisk together the olive oil, apple cider vinegar, Dijon mustard, honey, salt, and pepper to create the dressing.
3. Drizzle the dressing over the salad and toss gently to combine. Serve immediately.

Sweet Potato and Kale Salad with Maple Dressing

Ingredients:

- 2 medium sweet potatoes, peeled and cubed
- 4 cups kale, chopped and stems removed
- 1/4 cup red onion, thinly sliced
- 1/4 cup pumpkin seeds or sunflower seeds (optional)
- Salt and pepper to taste

For the Maple Dressing:

- 3 tbsp olive oil
- 1 tbsp maple syrup
- 1 tbsp apple cider vinegar
- 1 tsp Dijon mustard
- Salt and pepper to taste

Instructions:

1. Preheat the oven to 400°F (200°C). Toss the cubed sweet potatoes with olive oil, salt, and pepper. Roast on a baking sheet for 20-25 minutes, until tender and caramelized.
2. In a large bowl, massage the kale with a little olive oil and a pinch of salt to soften it.
3. Once the sweet potatoes are roasted, add them to the kale along with the red onion.
4. In a small bowl, whisk together the olive oil, maple syrup, apple cider vinegar, Dijon mustard, salt, and pepper to make the dressing.
5. Drizzle the dressing over the salad, toss gently, and garnish with pumpkin seeds (if using). Serve warm or at room temperature.

Arugula, Pear, and Pecan Salad

Ingredients:

- 4 cups arugula, washed and dried
- 2 ripe pears, thinly sliced
- 1/2 cup pecans, toasted
- 1/4 cup crumbled blue cheese (optional)
- 1/4 red onion, thinly sliced (optional)
- Salt and pepper to taste

For the Dressing:

- 3 tbsp olive oil
- 1 tbsp balsamic vinegar
- 1 tsp honey or maple syrup
- Salt and pepper to taste

Instructions:

1. In a large bowl, combine the arugula, sliced pears, toasted pecans, blue cheese (if using), and red onion (if desired).
2. In a small bowl, whisk together the olive oil, balsamic vinegar, honey, salt, and pepper to make the dressing.
3. Drizzle the dressing over the salad and toss gently to combine. Serve immediately.

Roasted Root Vegetable Salad

Ingredients:

- 2 large carrots, peeled and sliced
- 1 large sweet potato, peeled and cubed
- 1 parsnip, peeled and sliced
- 1 beet, peeled and cubed
- 2 tbsp olive oil
- Salt and pepper to taste
- 1 tbsp fresh parsley, chopped
- 1 tbsp fresh thyme leaves

For the Dressing:

- 3 tbsp olive oil
- 1 tbsp apple cider vinegar
- 1 tbsp Dijon mustard
- 1 tsp maple syrup
- Salt and pepper to taste

Instructions:

1. Preheat the oven to 400°F (200°C). Toss the carrots, sweet potato, parsnip, and beet with olive oil, salt, and pepper. Spread them evenly on a baking sheet.
2. Roast for 25-30 minutes, flipping halfway through, until the vegetables are tender and caramelized.
3. In a small bowl, whisk together the olive oil, apple cider vinegar, Dijon mustard, maple syrup, salt, and pepper to create the dressing.
4. Once the vegetables are roasted, toss them with the dressing and sprinkle with fresh parsley and thyme. Serve warm or at room temperature.

Broccoli and Feta Salad

Ingredients:

- 2 cups broccoli florets, steamed or blanched
- 1/4 cup red onion, finely chopped
- 1/4 cup sunflower seeds (optional)
- 1/2 cup crumbled feta cheese
- Salt and pepper to taste

For the Dressing:

- 3 tbsp olive oil
- 2 tbsp lemon juice
- 1 tbsp Dijon mustard
- 1 tsp honey
- Salt and pepper to taste

Instructions:

1. Steam or blanch the broccoli florets until bright green and tender but still crisp, about 2-3 minutes. Drain and cool under cold running water.
2. In a large bowl, combine the broccoli, red onion, sunflower seeds, and feta cheese.
3. In a small bowl, whisk together the olive oil, lemon juice, Dijon mustard, honey, salt, and pepper to make the dressing.
4. Pour the dressing over the salad and toss gently to combine. Serve chilled or at room temperature.

Apple Cider Vinegar Slaw

Ingredients:

- 4 cups shredded cabbage (green or purple)
- 1/2 cup shredded carrots
- 1/4 cup red onion, thinly sliced
- 1 apple, julienned (optional)

For the Dressing:

- 3 tbsp apple cider vinegar
- 1 tbsp olive oil
- 1 tsp honey
- 1 tsp Dijon mustard
- Salt and pepper to taste

Instructions:

1. In a large bowl, combine the shredded cabbage, carrots, red onion, and apple (if using).
2. In a small bowl, whisk together the apple cider vinegar, olive oil, honey, Dijon mustard, salt, and pepper to make the dressing.
3. Pour the dressing over the slaw and toss to combine. Let the salad sit for about 10 minutes to allow the flavors to meld. Serve chilled.

Poppy Seed Coleslaw

Ingredients:

- 4 cups shredded cabbage (green or a mix of green and purple)
- 1/2 cup shredded carrots
- 1/4 cup red onion, thinly sliced

For the Dressing:

- 1/2 cup mayonnaise
- 1 tbsp apple cider vinegar
- 2 tbsp honey
- 1 tbsp poppy seeds
- Salt and pepper to taste

Instructions:

1. In a large bowl, combine the shredded cabbage, shredded carrots, and red onion.
2. In a small bowl, whisk together the mayonnaise, apple cider vinegar, honey, poppy seeds, salt, and pepper to create the dressing.
3. Pour the dressing over the vegetables and toss to coat evenly. Serve chilled.

www.ingramcontent.com/pod-product-compliance
Lightning Source LLC
LaVergne TN
LVHW081330060526
838201LV00055B/2558